- Align and move
  a team of indiv.
  towards a bri.
  future

This is what I do...
- Align and move a team of
  individuals, capturing
  hearts & minds, towards common goals
  a brighter
  future.

↓ shorter

Align and move
  teams to
  achieve success

Audible —
"The Home of
Storytelling"

CONSULT YOUR WAY TO A FULL-TIME JOB

- Learn be an inside
  - Opportunity
  - Strengths
  - Challenges
- Competitive Landscape

- Culture & Company
- Capabilities of Leadership Team
- Skeletons in closet

Prefer Growth Mode or Trouble Mode
          Build or Fix
          ‿‿‿‿‿
        Problem-Solver

CONSULT YOUR WAY TO A FULL-TIME JOB

THE SECRET TRAIL GUIDE TO DISCOVER YOUR NEXT, BEST CAREER DESTINATION (AND GET PAID TO DO IT)

BY JOHN ARMS

Copyright ©2022 Unified Funnel Metrics LLC dba Voyageur U

All rights reserved. No part of this publication may be reproduced, distributed, or transmitted in any form or by any means, including photocopying, recording, or other electronic or mechanical methods, without the prior written permission of the publisher, except in the case of brief quotations embodied in critical reviews and certain other noncommercial uses permitted by copyright law. For permission requests, write to the publisher, addressed "Attention: Permissions Coordinator," at the address below.

ISBN: 979-8-9856340-1-3 (eBook)
ISBN: 979-8-9856340-0-6 (Paperback)

Library of Congress Control Number: 2022907255

Unless otherwise named, references to specific people have been either changed or created from multiple experiences.

Voyageur U
105 Elmwood Pl E
Minneapolis, MN 55419

For additional resources and coursework, visit:
www.VoyageurU.com

For everyone seeking to find their place in the new normal.
Never forget that you are more than enough.

Your value is in your wisdom.
Your value is in your objectivity.
Your value is in your scars.
Your value is in your viewpoint.
Your value is in your failures.

Table of Contents

Foreword..ii

Introduction...01

Chapter 1: Gambler's ruin. 02

Chapter 2: The reality of today's job market..06

Chapter 3: The other side of the table. 14

Chapter 4: Changing the rules of the game. 22

Chapter 5: Quantify your financial need. 32

Chapter 6: Determine the strength of your professional network........37

Chapter 7: Create your sales offer...42

Chapter 8: Easy sales techniques. 52

Chapter 9: Your business system. 58

Chapter 10: Managing your four-part schedule. 61

Chapter 11: Now...begin! 64

The trailhead for your independent career. 66

About John Arms...67

Foreword
by Steve Cadigan, Author of Workquake

The world of work today is filled with a great deal of uncertainty. In the past 25 years alone, more new industries have been created than in any 25 years in history. These new industries bring with them many unique opportunities such as the ability for people to forge new career paths. However, this radical pace of change in the career landscape has also put enormous strain on organizations. First, these new industries are attracting talent in record numbers, causing a spike in turnover. Second, most companies today are challenged to accurately forecast what skills they will require more than a few years ahead as every firm faces the constant pressure of digitally transforming themselves. All this has put significant strain on the hiring process for almost every organization. And as you will discover in this book, even before the pandemic, most recruiting functions were understaffed, under-resourced, and overburdened.

For better or worse, employers and employees both find themselves in an awkward and uncomfortable new reality where neither party is confident of the best path forward. I call this new reality a Workquake, and the COVID-19 pandemic has only served to throw kerosene on this fire. Most organizations were built to address a much slower pace of work and a much more predictable reality. We all know those days are over, but what does that mean for many who are seeking a new job...or maybe even a new career? If you are among the millions who wonder, 'what is next and how do I get there?' you have found the right resource. In this book, John Arms delivers a highly insightful, practical, and creative guide built to help you navigate the complex waters of job search today.

As John points out, many organizations have trouble hiring not because they don't care but because they are trying to keep up with a pace of change that they were not built to address. Not only do most companies have to hire faster than ever, but they also have to hire more new skills than they have ever hired before. This means you must take more control of your application process today. Simply tossing your hat into the ring won't cut it anymore because the "ring" has become a black hole of ghosting and employer non-re-

sponse. Therefore, you must build new strategies, approaches, and methods that optimize for a broken recruiting system. If you want to land your next full-time opportunity, or you want to explore a new direction today, you need to build a new game plan. You must take greater ownership of your career search and build a strategy that accounts for how the world has changed. The good news is that plan is laid out beautifully in the pages that follow.

As someone who has been recruiting for over 30 years in multiple world-class organizations, I must admit that the job interview is a highly flawed process that most of us lean on too heavily to make hiring decisions. Over my career, I have come to believe that the internship is the greatest interview process out there. It's essentially a "try before you buy/commit" process for both the candidate and the employer. Both parties get to test each other out to determine fit and compatibility. When we were growing LinkedIn, our close rate and our retention rate of internship hires was close to 95%. Ask any recruiter, and this is a phenomenally strong close rate when you are competing against the high-profile employer brands of Apple, Google, Facebook, and Twitter. The reason it was so high is because over a two-month internship process, we got to know the candidates really well, and they also had an excellent opportunity to try us on and see if our culture and environment suited their needs.

While some of you may not be college students, the good news is that the internship opportunity is still available to you, but it's referred to as something different. It's called being a consultant. That's right, consultant. If you think about it, consulting allows you to go into an organization, taste the culture, leadership, and environment, and learn if this is right for you without a long-term commitment. If you step back – isn't this so much better than doing a speed dating interview over a few days and then deciding after a few hours of meetings with just a few people if you want to commit years of your life to a company? That really feels suboptimal, yet sadly, this is the process for most companies today because it's the way "we have always done it."

If you are ready to build more career options for yourself in a landscape that feels complex and confusing, John provides you with templates and game plans to help you build and put into action a great strategy and game plan to consult. He breaks the process down into very actionable steps. But he also goes beyond just the practical – he helps you see yourself as if you were a company. He helps you become more aware of yourself, your skills, and your brand. While knowing your value may seem obvious, most of us struggle to talk about ourselves. Having helped hundreds of friends build resumes, I can tell you from experience that 95% of people struggle to tell the best stories about themselves. And this is why this book is infinitely valuable and why John's work here is so darn important. He takes you by the hand and literally walks you through this process as if he were your new career concierge.

Beyond simply providing you with a brilliant template to jump-start your consulting business, John is your wingman in this process, and his writing style is both humorous and comforting. He knows that changing our approach to finding a job can be scary for many of us. He breaks this process down and delivers his coaching with a unique blend of honesty and humor. He dispels myth after myth, helping you with his many templates, checkboxes, and step-by-step instructions. John essentially foolproofs the whole thing, allowing you to move into action mode quickly. Having more options has never been more critical in a world of rapid change, and this book gives you more options.

The power skill of the future is adaptability. If you implement the strategies and tactics in this book, you will be able to fish in a much larger ocean of career opportunities.

STEVE CADIGAN
Author of Workquake: Embracing the Aftershocks of COVID-19 to Create a Better Model of Working
https://stevecadigan.com/

Introduction

The job market is a shit show.

I'm sorry to say it so plainly, but it's true. I'll bet you've sat through dozens of networking meetings, applied for hundreds of jobs, and perhaps even made it to the final round of interviews on a few occasions. Yet it always seems like the right job is just out of reach. Adding to the soup are algorithms picking apart every word in your resume, fuzzy job descriptions you couldn't decode with an Enigma machine, and pay scales offering college grad pay for senior-level experience. By the time you actually receive an offer, it's for less money than you ever imagined you'd accept, at a company that doesn't excite you, for a boss that you know will drive you crazy.

But you need to take it, don't you? Your severance (if you had any) is running out, your savings are dwindling, and your self-confidence has taken a hard kick in the teeth. You've been at it for months with nothing to show for it. I am here to show you a different path.

You can consult your way to your next full-time job.

In this practical (and short!) book, I'm going to show you how to finally turn the system around in your favor. I'll show you how to earn money during your job search – essentially getting paid to interview at companies you may want to work for in the future. And if that sounds like a win to you, know that your potential employer sees it the same way. Just like you, they get to try before they buy, reducing the risk of a hire that's not a fit for their culture and goals.

Why now? Why this path?

The pandemic, the global shutdown, the great recession, and the great resignation have created a new reality for professional life – a reality tailor-made for consulting your way to a full-time job. It's the best kept "win-win" secret in the job market today.

Let's learn how.

01

Gambler's ruin.

Actually, you'd be better off playing the roulette wheel. The odds of landing on any single number are 37 to 1. Oddly, that's about the same chance you'll land an interview. But at least at the roulette wheel you'll get a fair chance.

The job market is like a casino: The odds are always stacked in favor of the house (the employer).

No matter how tempting it might be to imagine yourself as the big winner, the truth – *as you now know* – is far different. Most job-seekers lose when they pursue work in traditional ways. A 2019 poll showed that for every one corporate job posting, 250 people will apply. Only four to six people will even get an interview. Only one gets the job. That means 249 people get sent packing. How often has that happened to you?

I know what you're thinking. It's just a numbers game; if I apply for enough opportunities, I'm bound to get one. If I have a personal connection or an "in" with the hiring manager, I increase my chances. My former colleague just posted on LinkedIn that it took her only 12 days to land a new job – *a promotion!* – at the company I'm applying to. It's just a matter of time.

Unfortunately, hope is not a strategy. Having a good feeling about a job prospect is not a job offer. Simply applying for another job is like rolling the dice and watching your stack of chips dwindle in front of you.

But it can be difficult to internalize just how challenging your situation has become. Hope might not be a strategy, but it certainly springs eternal. I need to help you rip the bandage off. Right now. Ready?

How many of these statements describe your experience?

- You've met with several recruiters, but you haven't heard back from them.
- Online job marketplaces don't seem to generate any return for the amount of time they take.
- You constantly work on your resume but feel like it's hardly any different from one version to the next.
- All those "badges" you acquired to boost your skills aren't making any difference.
- You had a great conversation with the CEO or the hiring manager... but then heard nothing back.
- You've made it to the final round of interviews, only to be left waiting or told you were the runner up.
- You're doing everything right but nothing is working.
- You know every applicant tracking system (ATS) by heart.
- You've lost count of the number of positions you've applied for.
- When you "work around" the ATS, the hiring manager connects with you on LinkedIn...but doesn't pay any attention to your application.
- You are the only one who ever visits the website you created for yourself.
- Updates to your LinkedIn don't have any effect.

CONSULT YOUR WAY TO YOUR NEXT FULL-TIME JOB | **04**

- You've scoured social media for any negative mentions of yourself just to be sure.
- You've secured references, but they've never been contacted.
- Congratulations! You've been offered a job...at half of what you were making before.
- You've been looking for work for three months, six months, 12 months, or more.
- Professional life is moving on without you.
- Your savings are running out.
- Your severance (if you had any) is long gone.
- Friends and family no longer want to take your calls...
- ...and you're embarrassed to reach out because you have nothing new to tell them.
- You're tempted to drive an Uber, work at Starbucks, or just retire.
- You're ready to settle for any job that comes along.
- You're fighting with your spouse, your children, and your extended family.
- You've been diagnosed with depression.
- Your self esteem is wavering.
- You feel unwanted.
- You feel there must be something wrong with you.

I can tell you from personal experience working with hundreds of job-seekers that they feel most – *if not all* – of these statements describe them. Right now, you're probably thoroughly depressed. I'm sorry about that, but the truth hurts. Until you accept the facts of your situation, you won't be able to move forward. You need to accept the rules of the game...so that you can change them.

In this book, you'll learn how to re-stack the odds of the game in your favor.

It's time we went behind the scenes and learned the rules.

KEY TAKEAWAYS FROM CHAPTER 1

All your talent, hard work, dedication, and positive career progression only get you a seat at the gambling table. The odds of the "find a new job" game are stacked against you. Frankly, the odds are that you'll go broke before you hit the jackpot. You must accept that reality before you can have the courage to decide to play a different game.

Notes from the trail... Alex Hultgren

The illusion of stability in a full-time position is never called into question – as long as the system seems to be working for you (which could be for decades). But then, one day, when the morbid musical chairs game of corporate layoffs comes, you find yourself without a seat when the music stops. For the first time, you realize that the years of loyalty you had shown your company wasn't reciprocated.

So you have a choice: Do you want to jump back into a system that has already demonstrated that it sees you as a fungible cog in a wheel? Or would you rather take a step back and write your own playbook – one where you are able to fully articulate and demonstrate your value?

Let's be clear: Neither path is easy. But only a portfolio career gives you the control to chart your own path, on your terms.

ALEX HULTGREN
Chief Marketing Officer
CEO | Founder, Customers 1st Marketing
We help you delight your customers and find new ones!
M: 734-730-7648
ahultgre@gmail.com
LinkedIn.com/in/alexhultgren
customers1stmarketing.com

02

The reality of today's job market.

Two plus two equals...fish?

There's a great line in the movie *The Big Short* with Steve Carrell and Brad Pitt when fund managers are trying to make sense of collateralized debt obligations (CDOs) during the housing market bubble in the mid-2000s. People who watched the CDOs market found that it kept making less and less sense. Buying, selling, exchanging, and trading CDOs was an ever-growing pyramid scheme...and no one seemed to see it. Half of the banks who sold CDOs *didn't even know what they were selling.* Despite all logic, and the mounting evidence that the party couldn't last, the buying continued.

In a moment of frustration (as the market began to collapse) one fund manager exclaimed: "This makes no sense. It's like two plus two equals...fish!"

That's the job market today. It makes no sense. Everyone knows it, but companies keep hiring and employees keep applying just as they always have. Markets tend to do that when they are about to burst. Logic leaves the building, and for good reason. The **old rules** are being applied to a **new dynamic**. The result is always a meltdown of epic proportions.

It's time to bet against the job market. And to do that, you need to understand the pyramid scheme.

07 | JOHN ARMS

Most posted jobs aren't even jobs companies want filled soon. They're fishing expeditions. And those take time. It makes no sense, but that's the way it is.

You are likely to stay unemployed, on average:*

- Less than 5 weeks: 24.5%
- 5 to 14 weeks: 24.3%
- 15 to 26 weeks: 13.7%
- More than 26 weeks: 37.4%

If you're a senior-level professional, expect to be out of work for six to 12 months. Why is that?

1. There are more junior roles than senior roles – that may seem obvious, but most of us don't want to accept that. There are 50 junior-level jobs for every one senior-level job.
2. Many companies don't really know what they need, so they troll the waters for months on end. Many companies hold out hope that a unicorn will arrive to solve all of their problems. In their mind that unicorn is 35 years old with 36 years of experience, is happy to work 80 hours per week on a 75K annual salary, has five masters degrees, jogs 10 miles before breakfast, and has lunch weekly with Simon Sinek, Greta Thurnburg, Warren Buffet, and Serena Williams. There is no needle in that haystack, but they are looking anyway. Hiring is delayed until they come back to earth.
3. Everyone is flinching. Companies are very raw coming out of the pandemic. Nearly two years of survival mode has put a new lens on critical decision making, causing companies to be very, very careful about big decisions. They might hire junior talent quickly, but they move slowly when it comes to senior roles.

Shhh. The bots can hear you.

Finding new work has never been so humbling. Until recently, if you did good work, made career progress, and made a positive effect on your

---

* Source: Bureau of Labor Statistics, August 2021 (Seasonally-adjusted data)

company, you could tell a great story on your resume. Get that resume into the right people's hands and you stood a good chance at getting a new job.

But not anymore. Enter the bot that controls your destiny: the applicant tracking system (ATS).

The ATS is there to:

- Collect and process dozens (or hundreds, or thousands) of resumes/ applications for a single position, making it possible for human resources professionals to cast the widest possible net and find the best person for the job. (In reality, they provide the appearance of a wide net, but hiring managers often give their preferred candidates ways to circumvent the standard process.)
- Remove systemic bias from the application process, including race, ethnicity, gender identification, country of origin, educational background, credit scores, and other traditional factors used to prevent qualified candidates from getting an interview. (In reality, those factors remain, and now they're hard-coded into the algorithms.)
- Reduce liability by relying on a system, rather than a person. Often, companies can head off discrimination claims before they get started. (In reality, this is the big reason companies adopted them. They're like an insurance policy.)

Do any of those objectives of an ATS make it easier for you? No, of course they don't.

> In our own client research, we see 75 percent of them [clients] using an ATS of some kind, and of those, 94 percent say it improves their hiring process. That's a 180-degree difference from what candidates see – they tell us the hiring process is frustrating, fraught with bugs and glitches; they have to manually enter information in duplicate, and then – poof! They're never sure if it even is reviewed by a human," says J.P. Medved, a recruiting software specialist with Capterra, a software research and comparison service that helps businesses find the best software solution for their needs.*

---

* **Source:** CIO *Magazine*

These days most resumes are filtered and washed relentlessly through a crazy cycle of insanity. Let's follow your resume through a normal day.

1. You upload your resume for review for a job. It's only a matter of time before the CEO sees it, loves it, and hires you immediately, right? Wrong.
2. An ATS scans it for data. Yup, your future is now in the hands of bots and algorithms. Feeling reassured yet? Hold tight; it gets worse.
3. The ATS takes charge from here, filtering your data according to some rushed criteria on the other end. If by chance your resume pinged something and it got to a "save" pile to be looked at by a real human being (most don't), it will get a maximum of five minutes of attention by someone who is rushed and isn't exactly sure what the company is hiring for. (The CEO still hasn't seen your resume.)
4. Somehow your resume made it through the bots. Hooray! Wait, what's that? There are 75 others that made it too? That includes the one candidate the hiring manager had already hand picked. Dammit!
5. Fine. You'll just get a recruiter. They will champion you to victory, right? Not so much. Recruiters, god bless 'em, are having just as hard a time getting clarity on what businesses want as you are. Imagine how hard it is to find someone for a role that isn't clearly defined for people that want to pay 25% less in a market that is struggling to recover and hesitant to hire senior talent?

If you're over 40, things are about to get worse.

Your instincts about ageism are, largely, correct. It's a key form of discrimination that doesn't tend to get the attention others do.

"I wouldn't go as far as saying they discriminate," says Ashley Martin, an assistant professor of organizational behavior at Stanford Graduate School of Business. "But even fair-minded people seem to prioritize race and gender over age."

Martin adds: With older workers increasingly remaining in their jobs past the once-traditional retirement age of 65, whether because of a desire to keep working or a need for income, ambitious younger employees trying to move up in an organization sometimes see older workers as obstacles to advancement, or "opportunity blockers."*

Bottom line: You're unlikely to change this dynamic alone. You'll find it heartening to know that businesses are desperately seeking "wisdom workers," but they're unsure how to find them. The value of wisdom is beginning to bypass the value of grinding through hours in a day. Still, it's a slow process. Until the market fully converts to valuing wisdom workers over young grinders, you need to put yourself in a position to leverage your age, not be hindered by it.

KEY TAKEAWAYS FROM CHAPTER 2

The job market isn't just stacked against you, it's stacked against employers as well. Everyone knows that it's not delivering value to either party, but we're stuck in a vicious cycle with (seemingly) no way out. Accepting this fact is critical to finding creative ways to move forward.

---

* **Source:** *Stanford Business School, Journal of Personality & Social Psychology January 18, 2021*

Notes from the trail... Laura King

What senior career professionals need to know about working with a recruiter.

Okay, first things first: The number one thing professionals misunderstand is the difference between a recruiter *and an* agent.

A recruiter is paid by an end client to find candidates for an open position. We work on the client's behalf. Our job is to discover the best candidates for an open position through our own professional networks as well as through active searching for potential candidates.

To be clear, the company is not paying me to build my network. They only care about the specific requirements of their open position. So, although I'm always interested in building my network, I need to focus first on the open requisitions in my inbox.

An agent is paid by the job seeker (you) either up front or after you obtain employment. This person is there to uncover hidden career opportunities. Frankly, however, I have yet to find a recruiting firm that offers this type of service. 99% of search firms operate by the client funding the searches they conduct. If a firm does offer actual agents, it's only with the top of the top of the top talent. Sadly, they're not applicable for 99.99% of all professionals seeking work.

This is the heart of the confusion. I am a recruiter, not an agent. Most of the people you talk to will be recruiters as well.

Now that we have that cleared up, what's the best way to work with a recruiter?

First, know that if you're meeting with a recruiter, they are sizing you up in their mind. Most of us are "grading" you in our minds: Are you A+, A-, B, C, etc. level talent in your field? That sounds harsh, but it's true. Be honest with yourself about where you stand in the marketplace. Ask yourself how you compare on objective measures (years of experience, education, accomplishments) with others in your field.

The secondary things going through our minds as we meet with you are the answers to very practical questions: Is there an open position right now you could fit? Are you the type of person I tend to place? As a candidate, you can stand out by asking your recruiter what background and traits they look for in the kinds of professionals they place. That will help you know how likely it is that the recruiter will have a position to discuss with you in the future.

To help you answer that question before the meeting, do your homework. Explore the open positions on the recruiter's website. What are they most often recruiting for? Are you speaking with a recruiter that specializes in your field or is a generalist? Are they a senior recruiter (they'll likely recruit for more senior positions)? Earlier career recruiters tend to recruit for more junior positions. That's simply a feature of their professional network.

Next, it's important to set your expectations. Recruiters may have only 5-15 open positions at any given time, and only place a few candidates per month. (Surprised? Most people are!)

We cast a wide net because we need to present more than one "good fit" option to our clients. Bottom line: The likelihood that you are a match for an open position right now is low. You need to work ahead and develop the relationships for the long term.

But, beyond those tips, what can you do that will make you stand apart from 99 out of 100 potential candidates we talk to?

- **Give first:** One of the best ways to build that relationship is to help educate the recruiter about some facet of the talent market for your position. Or teach them something fun about you or your industry.
- **Be memorable:** We talk with dozens of people every day and hundreds of people in an average week. Make sure there's something about you (something positive or interesting!) that they can't forget.
- **Prepare for the conversation:** Have your elevator pitch refined in advance. Be clear about what you do and what value you bring to an employer. Quantified results are better than qualitative opinions!
- **Offer to help:** Is there anyone you can refer to the recruiter for an open position they've got? I always remember the people who help me.

And how about what not to do?

- **You can't let go of your big ego:** I can't tell you how many people look down on me as a professional and ask "Hey, what do you have for me?" That's...um...not the way to start the conversation.
- **Just because you're senior-level doesn't make you unique:** The truth is that lots of people have what you have. You need to be clear about how you are different or better.

And finally, a special note for "fractional" or consultant seekers.

Offering clients a "fractional" or "consulting" (aka, not full-time) solution is coming up in conversations more often – about 1 in 10 openings right now. This is especially true for companies that aren't quite sure what they want. If I refer you for an opportunity like that, you can help me by coming back to me later and debriefing me on what the company really needs from a new employee. That is hugely helpful!

If you keep these tips in mind, you're much more likely to have positive working relationships with recruiters as part of your career search.

Good luck!

LAURA KING
Practice Leader, SkyWater Search Partners
https://www.skywatersearch.com/

03

The other side of the table.

"Could a greater miracle take place than for us to look through each other's eyes for an instant?"
- HENRY DAVID THOREAU

It is not enough to recognize the challenge of your own situation, and then to realize there are thousands (tens of thousands, hundreds of thousands, millions) of other people in your exact same shoes.

You must also understand the perspective of an important gatekeeper on the path to your next full-time role: a human resources professional, working in a human resources department, doing things in a human resources kind of way.

In the interest of taking the meaning of Thoreau's advice to heart, we need to put ourselves in the other chair. What does it feel like to spend a day in the life of a talent acquisition (TA) manager, part of the broader HR team, in today's environment? In the interest of deepening your empathy well in order to advance your case with HR people, let's walk in their shoes for a day shall we?

Meet Amy.

8:00 a.m.

After pouring a cup of coffee and slipping by a water cooler discussion about both the Kardashians and fantasy football, Amy fires up her computer to start her day. The ATS shows six open positions, three pending positions (one that's complete, one that's not, and one from a hiring manager who doesn't know what he wants, marked URGENT), and 152 new applicants. LinkedIn has at least half of that volume. Indeed.com has shoved dozens into her email and a half-dozen envelopes and boxes from applicants occupy her chair. Out of all of that, only about one in five applicants have read the instructions and properly filled out the application.

8:01 a.m.

Email refresh: 37 new emails. 15 are relevant (a good ratio!).

8:30 a.m.

Time for a meeting. This one is a "quick 30-minute-er, no more I promise," says her boss. They discuss three topics – none of which are relevant to Amy's day-to-day right now: (1) the latest pandemic surge and how it will change return-to-office policies, (2) who is likely to push back on vaccine policies, and (3) Zoom etiquette after (yet another) "hot mic" incident. Is there any time to discuss the shortage of talent for engineering roles? No. Amy's boss needs to move on to another meeting.

9:00 a.m.

Meeting number two. This one is an internal interview with an executive at the company who is looking to hire for a senior role. In her first draft of what she's looking for, the executive asked for everything under the sun – someone who is C-level in both Finance and IT and has an MBA and 25 years of experience in our (niche) industry. The job budget is about $100,000 per year – $110,000 for a candidate with more experience. Ahhhh, the "unicorn." Actually, the stupid unicorn: a magical person with all the right talent and experience, who also remains ignorant to their own earning potential. Amy's initial feedback was to rewrite the request as two roles, (because, well, they are – one for Finance and one for IT) and to consider higher pay, as that budget rate is 50% under market rate. In the meeting Amy asks for the executive's edits. There are none. "Well, if we don't ask, we won't get it," states the executive, whom Amy will refer to in the future as the "Unicorn Whisperer" under her breath. It is abundantly clear that the Unicorn Whisperer has no idea what she wants and will keep interviewing until she finds it, dragging Amy along for the ride. The Unicorn Whisperer has already burned through 10 candidates, none of which are "right" for the position.

10:00 a.m.

Initial Zoom screenings for candidates. About 60% actually show up. The next two hours are fits and starts of work, interrupted with a never-ending stream of tech issues. *Can you hear me? I can hear you. Wait, now I can't hear you. Is it my earpods? Where's the volume? Is it a Mac thing? I'm on a Dell. Buster, shut the hell up! Sit. I said sit! Damn dog never sits. Do you have a dog?*"

10:30 a.m.

Oh, did the admin assistant forget to mention? Your 10:30 interview is in person, not virtual. There's no "passing time" to allow Amy to show up on time. She's seven minutes late to a 30-minute interview. And the next one starts, virtually (Amy hopes), at 11.

12:00 p.m.

There is no "lunch" today. Sorry. Lunch is a full hour of rewriting the company's virtual meeting policy. Draft 13. Maybe this is the lucky one. Why is Amy doing this? She's in talent acquisition, not policy development, right?

1:00 p.m.

Assembling an offer for an executive candidate. Word on the street is she already accepted another offer out east somewhere. Amy is reasonably certain she's wasting her time.

1:10 p.m.

A knock comes to Amy's office cubicle wall. It's the CEO here to express "concerns" about some aspect of the executive candidate's background that you thought had been settled a week ago.

1:12 p.m.

And...never mind. Confirmed. The candidate accepted another offer while Amy and her CEO were nitpicking that background thing.

1:13 p.m.

Emergency meeting to review the second choice candidates. All hands on deck. Mayday! Mayday! (Amy will never understand her CEO's ubiquitous Navy references.)

1:43 p.m.

The executive team determines that it's "just too risky" right now to bring on a new executive. Besides, the second-tier candidates all have "issues" that would need to be addressed. Amy sighs as three weeks of hard work spins down the drain, guaranteed to come back full-steam in a week with even more urgency – and yet, somehow, with even less clarity.

2:00 p.m.

Four back-to-back in-person interviews with senior candidates for a director-level role. Amy is privately terrified that they're savvy enough to sniff out that the position has no staff and no budget...and pays 20% below market. One candidate sniffs it out and leaves mid-interview. Just...walks out. That's the third time that's happened this month.

4:00 p.m.

A recruiter sends Amy an email marked URGENT – what's the status of the executive candidates he sent over? Those were the second choices for that job that just got nixed in the emergency meeting. But were they really nixed? Because it's 100% certain that the job will come back raging hot in a week. "What the hell do I tell him?" Amy whispers to her cubicle wall.

4:05 p.m.

Amy decides to pick up the phone, bite the bullet, and give the recruiter the news. Most recruiters are paid on placements, not time, and not the number of candidates presented. This is the fifth round the company has declined. The recruiter apologizes, but tells Amy he cannot work with her company any longer.

4:12 p.m.

Amy emails four other recruiters. In past years, Amy would have heard her phone buzzing within five minutes. Not this time. Does the word get around that fast?

4:30 p.m.

Time to get ready for a new college graduate information session that starts at 6 p.m. on campus. Maybe there's time for a quick bite at Wendy's on the way to the university? Does Wendy's serve wine?

Obviously, this isn't a realistic day for a talent acquisition professional. Most days are worse. And we haven't even talked about onboarding and human resources. Yikes.

It is the norm, not the exception, that talent acquisition professionals are trapped in a daily whirling swirl of vague expectations, poor offers, impatient people, and overwhelming technology meant to make their lives "easier" (ha, ain't that rich?). The only thing worse than an average day in HR? Having to accomplish the same task without an HR professional to help. Imagine the poor CEO who has to find talent all by herself? It's not hard to imagine; thousands of business leaders have to tackle this every day, which brings us back to empathy. Now that you have a deeper understanding of life in their shoes, what do you do with this knowledge?

KEY TAKEAWAYS FROM CHAPTER 3

If you can provide a solution that simplifies the situation and reduces risk for the other side of the table at the same time, YOU WIN.

1. Think your application is good? Review the specific requirements and write it again. Every time you sharpen it, you make Amy's job easier.
2. Be sure to email Amy five times a day, call her and leave long voice-mails "just checking in." Actually, don't do that. Irritating HR only makes their life harder. That is not a list you want to be on. Instead,

follow the instructions they gave you for follow-up. In the absence of instructions, a good rule of thumb is one email follow-up five days after you submit your materials, and a request to connect on LinkedIn. No more.

3. Give them options! Worried about a full-time hire? Suggest that the company bring you on in a fractional (part-time) capacity for three months. In that time, the company will save money and develop a clearer picture of what it needs in that role. And why not keep the position open in the meantime?

We'll talk about #3 next.

Notes from the trail... Lorri Anderson

Did you see a job posting online that would be perfect for a consulting role (instead of a full-time position)? Are you considering trying to "sell" a talent acquisition manager (TA) or human resources partner (HR) on that change?

Before you can start the "sales" process, you must work to overcome three key fears. (And they're big ones, so take your time!)

1. *First, the biggest one: Don't assume TA/HR professionals have a comfort level with contract documents like the one you're using for your consulting business. They've learned (through painful experience!) that everything that looks, smells, or feels like an employment contract must go through a legal review. That said, TA/HR professionals recognize that the market is evolving and are working to build their own contract review skills.*

2. *Their second fear (hassle? hurdle?) – if they haven't used independent contractors in the past – is that they'll need to think through the policies and procedures put in place for employees and determine which, if any, apply to the contractor. I'm thinking about things like the company's anti-harassment policy or, if the individual will work inside their building from time to time, what they will need access to and what must they sign off on. Once TA/HR determines which, if*

any, policies apply, they'll probably need to create a new version of the documentation so it's clear there's no intent to treat the individual as an employee. For TA/HR, it's a brain-bending exercise and one that will take some time and effort, even if the end decision is to do nothing.

3. And there's a third potential fear: TA/HR professionals might feel like they'll be cut out of the loop. Because the "deal" happens between the candidate (consultant), the hiring manager, and finance/accounts payable, the TA/HR professional may not be privy to information they feel a need to know. I think there are benefits to keeping TA/HR in the loop, which may be apparent as you read on.

Made it past these hurdles? Great! For those charged with finding the best talent, there are many advantages to considering a consultant:

- A growing talent pool outside the business-as-usual recruiting pool (which happens to be shrinking) and top talent that isn't available for full-time work, due to converging forces:
  - Demographics
  - Baby Boomers who are transitioning out of the workforce
  - Younger employees who aren't interested in 40-hr/wk. jobs
  - Health insurance is increasingly available outside traditional employer-provided plans
  - Accessibility due to technology and acceptance of remote work
- Talent that can solve for the issue when there is one job that requires multiple, sometimes mutually exclusive skill sets – a common dilemma in smaller, growing businesses.
- The ability to fill an interim gap (after the departure of a key person or until growth allows for a full-time hire) – Some fractional candidates could be interested in the full-time role when it becomes available and will already be trained. If they're not interested or chosen for the full-time role, they can ease the onboarding process for a new traditional hire. Either path takes the heat off the TA for filling a key full-time role quickly.
- Immediate availability – ready to hit the ground running within days or weeks, compared to weeks or months.

- *Traditional employment risks are nearly non-existent: no risk in the selection process; no potential discrimination claims, no-fault severability; agility to handle peaks and valleys in the workload; and low hassle to "downsize" when not needed.*
- *Work product/outcomes/expectations are all clear and documented in writing. (BONUS: provides a way for the organization to improve their leaders' skills at performance management!)*

Additional advantages of consultants for the business overall:

- *Top talent is available to take the business to the next phase of success.*
- *Independent perspectives from outside the business bring in new ideas and viewpoints.*
- *Provides an effective way to scale a function, using fractional talent to build infrastructure that will be needed as the business grows.*
- *Lower overhead with higher efficiency – higher rates are offset by focused work – only what the business needs, when it needs it, and no paying for those extended water cooler discussions, time reviewing personal email, or the hundreds of other things full-time employees are doing during their 40-hour workweeks.*
- *Additional costs the company doesn't have to incur:*
  - Benefits
  - Training
  - Payroll taxes
  - PTO/holidays

Bottom line: Not every talent acquisition or human resources professional (or company) will be ready to begin considering consultants as a standard replacement for full-time employees, but if you can navigate the fears and obstacles, TA/HR professionals can be a great resource for aspiring consultants!

LORRI ANDERSON
HX Coaching & Consulting | A Better Human Experience
www.linkedin.com/in/lorrianderson
e: anderson_lorri@yahoo.com
m: 763.607.4139

04

Changing the rules of the game.

"The very definition of insanity is doing the same thing over and over again and expecting a different result."

- **ALBERT EINSTEIN** might have said this, but he probably wasn't the first, and he definitely will not be the last

Consulting your way to your next job is the ultimate career hack.

Why did we spend so much time talking about the situation you (and millions of others) find yourself in, the current state of the market for senior-level job-seekers, and the view from the talent acquisition professional's perspective? Because hidden within the problems we covered is a very simple solution.

Why walk into a brick wall when you can stroll around it?

Organizations of all sizes – *but especially small to mid-sized companies* – desperately need *your talent, wisdom, objectivity, and experience* to take their business to the next level. The problem is they have no idea how to access it. They need the talent, but aren't (yet) in the position to afford it.

But to get to the position where they can afford it, they need your talent. Catch-22? Chicken and the egg? Pick a metaphor. Hiring full-time is too much of a gamble for companies today. And it's up to you to prove to them there is another way.

The solution is obvious, isn't it? Allow your next boss to *try before they buy.*

In the following chapters, we're going to teach you how to use consulting as a way to flip the script on the job search. Never again will you ask an employer to take a chance on you. You're going to skip the guesswork and go directly to delivering tangible value in a contained time frame for a less-risky amount of money – that they can walk away from at any time.

Guess what? They often won't want to. But *you* might. More on that later.

Do you ever wish you could get paid to search for jobs and send a bill after the interview? That's what this is, except that the interview is three months long.

So, how do you deliver value? Before we get into the specifics, let's summarize the shift in mindset you must make based on the fears and anxiety embedded in their point of view:

Their anxiety	Your solution
Hiring you as a full-time employee is too expensive.	Your price will be 33% of the cost of a full-time hire. (No worries, you'll be "interviewing" with more than one client, and only working on their business for a fraction of your time.)

Their anxiety	Your solution
They're worried you won't be able to step in and solve the problem they have right away.	Ha! As opposed to letting it sit and fester? Because that's what has been happening. Your wisdom is the exact ointment the problem needs right away. Know that all open positions have an underlying problem the organization has been trying to solve. That's why they wrapped the problem into a full-time role. It's the default answer. Use your experience to discover the problem and offer to solve just that...without the full-time role.
Benefits are expensive.	You will handle those on your own during the contract period. Don't worry about it. We can talk about that after three months.
They don't know exactly what they need.	No problem. You've been down this road before. You're "senior" level, right? You will take on the job of defining that for them over a very short period of time. In the old days you'd give that away for free during the interview process. Now you'll be paid for it.
Hiring a full-time employee is what they always do.	Correct. And you are not alone. That's what most companies do. But the batting average for that keeps getting worse. Good people stay for less time, and bad people stay forever. That's the new normal. Knowing that, "What does it hurt to try me out for a month or two while you carefully navigate the new normal?" Nothing. It's all upside for them. You've given them an out they've been hoping for but couldn't see until you opened the aperture for them. And you're solving their problems pronto.

Their anxiety	Your solution
You might be working for three other companies. They want you "dedicated" to them.	Consultants *always* work for more than one firm. That's a feature, not a bug. Because of this, consultants and fractional professionals bring more wisdom, objectivity, experience... and, heck, even a fresh network to help you see different ways to solve problems. On top of that, if you were full-time, your time would be spent working for three other "companies." The first "company" would be your actual job. The second "company" would be the commute back and forth, water cooler chit chat, birthday parties, and paid sick days. The third "company" would be solving things you are not suited to solve, but, because you are a warm body here full-time, you tackle them anyway. Hiring you for a few months gets the employer 100% of what it needs to solve its problems with zero waste.

That's what they get out of it.

How about you? What do you get out of it?

1. **Paid.** You get money. And you get it a lot sooner than you would if and when a full-time job comes. Cash is king. Your win here is you mitigate (or eliminate) the drain on your savings while you are in transition.
2. **Confidence.** You're back in the game. You're doing what you do best. You're solving stuff. You're wanted and needed. Your blade is getting sharper. (As opposed to the drawn out dullness of waiting for a full-time role.)
3. **Wisdom.** Another set of challenges. Another situation to learn from. New people to engage with. Your worldview widens every day. Which is better? Waiting six months for a new job during a painful transition period, or learning new stuff fast?

4. **A bigger network.** Your new boss, co-workers, investors, board, their vendors, and partners – even though it's a shortened time frame, your new role is a gold mine of valuable new connections. This is a networking dream.
5. **Control.** Be careful. You may just like consulting full-time after all. Well, maybe you do, maybe you don't. Either way you have far more control of your career now. The options are yours.
6. **Breathing room.** Consulting for a short period will give you the financial breathing space you need to make the *best* possible decision, not the *first* possible decision.

Does this sound different from the advice you're getting about your job search right now? Yeah, it sure is. That's because most advice you'll hear falls into two categories:

1. Find a new job by "trying harder" or "working smarter." (That's what got you to this point, isn't it?)
2. Say, "Heck with it!" and consult full time. (What if you don't want to be on your own forever?)

This is the third way: door number three.

It's a different path – one that gives *everyone* (you and potential employers) exactly what they need.

KEY TAKEAWAYS FROM CHAPTER 4

This will be easier than you think! You have all the skills to consult; you simply need a plan and some help with the details. That's what the next chapters will show you.

1. Take some pressure off of yourself. You don't have to solve the next 15 years of your career at the moment. Breathe a little.
2. You're more valuable than you think. Your wisdom, objectivity, experience, and, yes, even your failures, are extremely valuable. Even better, they are yours and yours alone, unique only to you. No other person has them. You are your own niche market.
3. There's money on the table. Is it the full meal deal you're thinking of? No. But is it more than enough to pay your bills and tuck some away? Absolutely. Is it money that can turn into more money later? Absolutely. Is it money that comes sooner than the money that would come with a full-time job 12 months down the road? Absolutely.

BONUS SECTION: What is NOT important?

The problem we see with most independent consultants is that they follow well-meaning advice they get online, and they find themselves stuck in the planning phase.

- What is my target audience?
- What companies are in that market?
- How will I handle different geographies?
- How will I set my rate? Should I have multiple rates?
- Will I accept pro bono work?
- What additional certifications do I need?
- What classes should I take?
- What is the unique process I will offer to my clients?
- What's my logo going to look like?

- What's the best business name?
- How much time should I spend on my website?
- Where should I get my new photo?
- What accounting software should I get?

There's nothing wrong with answering these questions. But they just don't matter that much right now.

The issue is that you risk forgetting your goal: You are doing this as a bridge to your next full-time career, not a permanent transition to a "fractional executive" life. If you want to do that, or decide later that you do, you'll have plenty of time to circle back and plan out a long-term strategy. And, frankly, the experience of having a couple of clients will deeply inform that plan!

Psychologically, it's easy to plan. It feels good. It feels like you're making progress. It feels like you're working smarter, not harder. But be honest with yourself. The only way you get true traction is by putting yourself out there. It's scary, but you can do it. We'll show you how.

Until then, your philosophy should be this: What's the fastest and easiest way to earn consulting income while I look for a full-time job?

Here are some (more productive) answers for this stage in your professional life:

- **Question:** What is my target audience? Answer: *The people in your professional network who could hire you.*
- **Question:** What companies are in that market? Answer: *The companies they work for.*
- **Question:** How will I handle different geographies? Answer: *If you can, stick close to home. You'll want the benefit of deeper face-to-face interactions even if the role is virtual.*
- **Question:** How will I set my rate? Should I have multiple rates? Answer: *Pick a number between $100 and $300 per hour and be done. No one will care about your rate; they'll care about the monthly fee – which, by the way, should start at $2,500 per month minimum.*

Remember, that works out to about four to six hours a week for you, and an annualized rate of $30,000 per year for your client. That level of commitment should give you plenty of time to keep up your job search, and it's cost-effective for them.

- **Question:** Will I accept pro bono work for your favorite non-profit? *Answer: Not unless you can afford it. If you're reading this book, the answer is probably no.*
- **Question:** What additional certifications do I need? *Answer: You have everything you need.*
- **Question:** What classes should I take? *Answer: None.*
- **Question:** What is the unique process I will offer to my clients? *Answer: Whatever you've been doing in your career. Don't worry about inventing something new right now. If it happens during the course of a consulting contract, great.*
- **Question:** What's my logo going to look like? *Answer: You shouldn't create one.*
- **Question:** What's the best business name? *Answer: Your name, LLC. That's it. See Chapter 9 for legal details.*
- **Question:** How much time should I spend on my website? *Answer: None. Your LinkedIn profile is enough.*
- **Question:** Where should I get my new photo? *Answer: Don't, unless your current photo is more than five years old. In that case, take it against a white wall with your smartphone. Got kids? Have them do it.*
- **Question:** What accounting software should I get? *Answer: None. A spreadsheet with your income and expenses will do just fine for tax time. Talk with your accountant for details on what information they'll want from you at the end of the year. See Chapter 9.*

Notes from the trail... Roger Scherping

I had just worked my way out of yet another job as the Entrepreneurial Operating System (EOS®) Integrator at a small company. It usually takes me two years to get a company straightened out and profitable again – and then I generally find myself looking for another job. In 2017, I realized that it was just too difficult to keep finding a new job every two years. I realized that I needed a better business model.

A friend told me that companies cannot afford a full-time EOS Integrator unless they had at least 50 employees, and that made me realize that if I wanted to keep doing what I enjoy with small companies, then I needed to become a consultant. As a consultant, instead of going from employed to unemployed, I would maintain a group of fractional clients that would come and go over time.

I had never imagined myself as a consultant. Like most people, I wanted the security of a steady paycheck. So I weighed the pros and cons of becoming a consultant. I thought I could make more money working three days a week than I had previously made working five. I would be in control, choosing the clients I wanted to work with and the hours I wanted to work. Of course, I would need to find clients, but I am a good networker and EOS is very popular in the Twin Cities, so I decided to jump into the gig economy.

Four years later, I will never go back to being an employee. It took me just three months before I told my wife that I should have quit my job years ago. I love working with different clients in multiple industries. I enjoy the freedom of being able to take some personal time in the middle of the day if I want to. I have been able to find clients through networking and the effective use of a website and LinkedIn. Today, I make more money consulting with clients I like while working fewer hours than I did earlier in my career.

As a consultant, I bring to my clients many years of experience at different companies and across multiple industries. Looking back, I think my career has been a series of two-year consulting projects. As a result, I bring a breadth and depth of experience that my clients simply do not have. I also enjoy the fact that I no longer do the work. Instead, I advise, counsel, coach, instruct, teach, and guide. Earlier in my career I could not have done what I do now. It took many years to develop my unique background, and now I am able to share what I know and have a big impact at my small-company clients.

Do I worry about Imposter Syndrome? Not really. I sometimes work in an industry that I am not intimately familiar with, and there is a chance I might unknowingly say something ignorant. I just try to stay open and honest. I am always quick to admit when I do not know something. I ask lots of questions and never try to fake it. It also helps that at this point in my career I am guided much more by my gut than ever. Even if I do not know an answer, I usually have a good hunch that comes from years of experience. I get a great deal of confidence from the knowledge that I've "been there, done that."

I am a part of that group of fractional executives whose white hair proudly speaks for our many years of business experience. Retirement is out there on the horizon for me, and I could not be in a better place right now. While my wife will leave her job and become retired overnight, I can choose to reduce my number of clients and slide gradually into retirement, working as much as I want as I transition to full retirement

ROGER SCHERPING
roger@rogerscherping.com
Cell 651-247-1993
I was an Integrator before the book was written.™

05

Quantify your financial need.

"You do the math. You solve one problem... and you solve the next one... and then the next. And If you solve enough problems, you get to come home."
  - MATT DAMON in *The Martian*

There's nothing quite like seeing your need in dollars and cents, so that's where we start. Instead of asking "How many clients can I handle?" and "What should I charge?", it's more useful to understand what return you must see on your investment. Yes, we'll answer those questions; but if you're reading this, you're likely under financial stress or you will be soon. Until we address the elephant in the room, we can't move forward.

Let's walk through an example. You can adjust the numbers for your own situation.

Clara was laid off from her job as an IT manager for a mid-sized manufacturing and distribution company. She earned $110,000 per year with a 401k match and full health benefits. Her exit package was generous: six weeks salary plus full benefits during that time, though she would no longer receive a 401k match. Her first step is to collect all of her assets to determine how long she could maintain her current lifestyle without working:

Category	Savings Amount
Liquid savings accounts	$4,250
Severance package (cash)	$13,750
Severance package (health benefit value)	$5,500
401k retirement account	$156,000
Total	**$179,500**

At first glance, this looks good. Clara could easily go a year (or more) without any income. However, look more closely. The health benefit is not cash in the "I can spend that" sort of definition. It simply means that Clara avoids that expense during the next couple of months. What's more, taking loans from a retirement account not only typically incurs early-withdrawal penalties, but also sacrifices long-term financial stability.

In reality, Clara has about four months of runway before she's out of reserves. We calculate that by adding her severance package to her savings, and then assuming she will need to purchase healthcare on the open market for the fourth month.

A typical job search for a senior position can take up to a year or more, so Clara is faced with eight months of income and health insurance premiums to make up. Keep in mind, we're not accounting for other financial com- mitments (student loans, elder care, etc.), and many people aren't as well off as Clara.

In our scenario, let's assume that Clara tightens her belt and reduces expenses such as her gym membership, extra contributions to savings accounts, charitable contributions, and the like. Many people discover that they can adjust their lifestyle...to an extent. Clara is no different.

Here's where she ended up:

Expense	Amount (mo.)	Decision
Mortgage	$1,650	No change
Car payment	$450	No change
Gas and upkeep	$150	Reduce to $100
Student loan repayment	$150	Reduce to zero (forbearance)
Groceries	$1,000	No change
Gym membership	$150	Eliminate
Charitable contributions	$250	Eliminate
Utilities	$250	No change
Insurance	$350	No change
Discretionary	$500	Reduce to $250
Total	**$4,900**	**$4,050**
Reduction	**$850**	**-17.3%**

Hmm. Notice something? Reductions in discretionary spending usually don't have the impact you hope they will. That's certainly the situation with Clara. When you count the increase in expense because she'll need to purchase health insurance (or go without), the overall impact of cost savings is minor. In this example, all these savings won't even buy Clara another month.

Yes, I recommend that you trim expenses; but no, cost savings alone usually is not enough.

Put simply, Clara needs to come up with a plan to replace her salary. The amount she can replace will determine how long her savings can stretch – giving her the runway to find her next full-time job.

Situation ($4,050/mo in expenses)	Runway (months)
Option 1: Use only "liquid assets" – $18,000 (current savings + cash severance)	4
Option 2: Add one consulting project at $2,500 per month (about four hours per week)	About 7
Option 3: Add two consulting projects at $2,500 per month each (about eight hours per week) for a total of $5,000 per month in revenue	Indefinite* *Depending on your tax situation*

Based on her monthly expenses, Clara can stretch her savings nearly twice as far with only *one* new consulting client! Is that worth investing four hours per week? I'll bet Clara thinks so! What's more, if Clara takes on another client (investing about one day per week), she can wait until the right job finds her.

Obviously, there are a few mitigating factors:

- If the projects are larger or smaller, the runway calculation changes. A small number of large projects are easier to manage but harder to secure. More numerous, smaller projects are easier to sell, but harder to manage alongside a job search.
- $2,500 is a happy medium – it equals about $30,000 per year, which is less than the salary of a new college graduate in many industries. For many organizations, that number is small enough to be inconsequential in their planning, but large enough to be meaningful for you.
- You'll need to earn more than you think, and that's based on your tax situation. Plan for at least 25% more than you believe you'll need so that you can cover any tax liability. (See Chapter 9 for a STRONG reminder to communicate with an accountant for tax advice.)

The norm of full-time work in the past 75 years feels like a catch-22 sometimes. If you have a full-time job, you can lose it (damned if you do). If you don't have a full-time job, you'll lose your healthcare and retirement savings (damned if you don't).

Consulting your way to a full-time job gives you an option to not be damned at all. You get the opportunity to work around the norm to your favor and find a work situation that works, finally, to your benefit.

KEY TAKEAWAYS FROM CHAPTER 5

The mindset shift you'll need to make anchors to financial realities. It has to. Though consulting is exciting, full of freedom and opportunity, and gives you far more control than just one full-time job, you still need to anchor yourself into your finances to make it work.

1. You need to do the math on your finances to make consulting work. Keep it simple. Use Clara's example in this chapter to get yours pinned down.
2. Each consulting gig gives you more time to find the right fit in your next full-time role. Even one consulting project doubles the amount of time you can hold out before that full-time job offer comes.
3. Each consulting project keeps your fingers out of your savings till. It only takes one consulting gig to help you avoid the situation where you dip into (and exhaust) your savings, giving you immeasurable peace of mind.

06

Determine the strength of your professional network.

"A friend is one who overlooks your broken fence and admires the flowers in your garden."
- UNKNOWN

As professionals, we've all heard about the need to network. However, many of us simply haven't invested the time and energy necessary to build the connections that will sustain us during a job search, open the doors to other people in decision-making roles, and uncover consulting opportunities. Bluntly speaking, when your job was stable for years, there didn't seem to be a pressing need for it. Even more bluntly, the job you have, or had, didn't allow much time for it. Even bluntly-er, what if your coworkers and boss see you suddenly getting active in networking, particularly on LinkedIn? That's three strikes against networking.

If that's you, don't worry. You're not alone. And you can fix it. But you need to start right now.

First, let's get a sense of where your network stands today. We'll use Timothy as our example. He's been a senior finance professional for the past 18 years and has built a reasonable network. Based on his connections on LinkedIn (1,024 as of today), let's use some simple rules of thumb to see how likely it will be that he can "mine" his network for the opportunities he needs:

Voyageur U Networking Power Law:

For every 1,000 **connections** you have...
100 will be willing to have a **conversation** with you...
10 will be **useful** in your search...
And 1 will result in a tangible consulting or job **opportunity**.

The problem is, you can only guess at who those people are when you start.

What does that mean for Timothy? He has 1,024 connections on LinkedIn, meaning that he has a means to communicate with that many people.

For the sake of this example, we can ignore people who are not on LinkedIn or some other social network. What you're interested in is their connection to others more than their individual opportunity potential, so social networks are critical. More on that in a moment.

Timothy fits our Networking Power Law almost exactly. It's likely he has at least one consulting opportunity hidden in his network right now! That's great news – *and gives him a boost of confidence* – but what if his situation is like Clara's, and he needs *two* opportunities to carry him through? Is Timothy out of luck?

No!

Here's a way to quickly increase the size of your network.

Remember that the Networking Power Law states that 100 people will be willing to have a conversation with you. That doesn't mean they are all created equal! Haven't you noticed that some people in your network are simply more connected than others? More outgoing? More engaged? Your instincts are correct. Those people drive value for themselves and others through their connections. You can tap into their networks to quickly expand yours.

With that in mind, Timothy quickly scans his 1,024-person network. He discovers the following:

Total people: 1,024
Total people over 500 connections: 457
Total people over 1,000 connections: 98
Total people over 5,000 connections: 24
Total people over 10,000 connections: 3

Bingo!

How to hack the Networking Power Law

Now Timothy has a prioritized list of people to reach out to. Of course, those three people with over 10,000 connections might be the most valuable, but they might be busy (or overwhelmed with requests). His strategy should involve reaching out with a personal, but honest, message about why he's reaching out. He'll likely be surprised with the response...at least from a few of them.

However, his focus should be on those connections in the 1,000+ to 5,000+ range – they are strong networkers, but unlikely to have "professional celebrity" status (those with that status have needed to filter their requests long ago). Of those 122 connections, Timothy was surprised with the positive response. Not only were they able to help connect him with people who could have consulting needs and "hidden" (unposted) job opportunities, but, more importantly, they connected him with other "master connectors" like themselves, dramatically increasing the "useful" searches in the Networking Power Law.

The Secret to Networking

In the first part of this chapter, we shared the numbers part of networking. It is indeed a numbers game. We also shared some dynamics of networking. Not all connections are created equal. Those are the what and the who of networking. Now we have to talk about the how. Remember these four words, tattoo them on your ankle, write them in permanent ink in your journal, and etch them in your brain.

It's. Not. About. You.

That's the big secret. You want it to be about you. You even need it to be about you. But for networking to work for you, it simply can't be about you. We have a saying within our Voyageur U community: "This is a place to help and be helped." One begets the other, in that order. The hundreds and hundreds of successful consultants in the Voyageur U community prove this to be true each day. The more you help others, the more you receive help from others. To some this may sound like a warm fuzzy, easily heard and forgotten. To others this may sound like some sort of social duty that is adjacent to a business purpose but not square in the target. Believe me, helping others is the exact bullseye of networking. Let's unpack that because on the surface it makes absolutely no sense. Old truths begin to flood the mind as you contemplate networking:

"Put your own mask on first."
"You don't get what you don't ask for."
"The squeaky wheel gets the grease."

You'll do better by putting those out of your mind. When your networking begins with you, it is doomed from the start. You simply have to make it about others for networking to boomerang around to benefit you.

Here are four ways to network and make it not about you:

- **Post on LinkedIn:** "If anyone needs a professional viewpoint with deep experience in (your skill set), I am available. Here is my email. No charge." (This is your "1,000" number.)

- **Note to new LinkedIn connections**: "Good to connect with another professional in our industry. If you ever need a viewpoint on (your skill), feel free to shoot me a note. Here is my email." (This is your 100 number)
- **Do a small project**: Offer your skill set to a consultant you already know who doesn't have the skill set you have.
- **Email your connections**: "Hey all, I'm consulting and have some free time. If you need a brain with my experience to pick, shoot me a note. Happy to help."

Here's why it works. People refer genuinely nice people. It's the only referral we can give in good conscience. When your networking is anchored in sharing your experience and helping others, the referrals come your way. I suppose I could have put this another way and made it a shorter lesson: How likely are you to refer a self-centered asshole to someone? Not *very*.

KEY TAKEAWAYS FROM CHAPTER 6

We are shifting from *growing in place* in our careers – having a job for years, then having them pay for your MBA, moving up the ladder, and focusing on their business' priorities – to *growing in motion* – actively networking, growing a community around you, offering your help to others, and focusing on your own business priorities.

1. It's a process. There is math involved in networking. Most people who have over 10 years of experience in business have more than enough people in their orbit to support a consulting effort.
2. Not all connections are equal, but they are all awesome. A CEO connection may not have a ton of connections, but the ones they have are probably very high value. A mid-level VP may not have a lot of influential connections, but they may have a lot of influence in their category.
3. Networking is not about you; it's about how you can help. Help first, even if you don't feel like you can. It'll come back to you. I promise.

07

Create your sales offer.

"If you got a problem, yo, I'll solve it."
- VANILLA ICE

For most people, "selling themselves" is the single most terrifying part of the job search. On one level, it feels like bragging. That's not a natural habit for most people.

But beyond the feeling that talking about yourself feels distasteful, it's often hard to put the value you offer into words. Most people struggle to articulate their value, and when they do, they struggle even more to keep it brief, to the point, and focused on what the buying party needs (not what the seller/you can offer). When faced with the chance to sell themselves, most people ramble on about themselves. All that rejection you hear about in the sales process makes a bit more sense now, doesn't it?

Feeling called out?

Don't worry; we can fix that.

A fear of selling themselves stops the majority of people from taking advantage of the opportunities sitting directly in front of them.

Put simply, you need to get over your fear of sales. We're going to show you the skills you need to reframe your misconceptions about sales in three key areas:

1. Sales is not about bragging or ego; it's about matching price and value.
2. Sales is not about more options; it's about fewer (better) choices for customers.
3. Sales is not about rejection; it's about attraction.

Who are you?

In your consulting business, you must have a clear way for people to understand very quickly what you do and what value you add. The simpler, the better. The clearer, the better. The more value-focused, the better. The shorter, the better.

In this example, Martha is a senior-level finance executive. She's played the role of CFO at a smaller company, but more often in her career she has been a VP of finance or finance director. The following is Martha's attempt to figure out the value she offers.

First things first: The title does not matter. She could substitute "CFO" with "finance director" in the following statements and they would mean the same thing. Remember this: Your job search cares about titles; clients care about results.

Let's see where Martha started in articulating her value...and where she ended up.

Good	Better	Best
I am a CFO consultant.	I am a fractional CFO.	I fix your broken books.
This is accurate, but not ideal. Business owners may not have the best impression of a "consultant" – they may have had poor experiences.	Fractional implies something more – a commitment to the business over a period of time. This also allows you a way to talk about the "pay for what you need" value.	Notice how the first two talk about what you are, and this one talks about the value you provide? It also helps people know when to refer you when a colleague mentions that problem. This is what we call "knowing your superpower." Martha nailed hers here.

How do you package what you do?

Most first-time consultants overestimate how much work it will be to create a business proposal for the services they'll perform for a client. Don't worry. If you're an experienced professional, you know exactly the actions the client needs done and how to do them, don't you? You do. It's simply the act of packaging those actions into a proposal the client can sign off on that trips you up. Let's simplify that process for you right now.

Using Martha as our example again, how would she package her offering based on a conversation she had with the CEO of a small manufacturing firm?

Proposal Section	Example Response	Rationale
Specific problem you're solving	Your recent audit revealed inconsistency in revenue recognition and inventory calculations over the past year. My job is to clean up the past three years of financial records and set processes in place to prevent the issue from recurring.	This is where you restate the specific problem the client wants you to solve. It shows that you listened and makes it clear what you're there to do. Remember, you're not an employee – there are no "other tasks as assigned" ...unless they're willing to pay you to do that.
Specific tasks	<ul><li>Perform a three-year audit</li><li>Consult with former CPA firm for their input</li><li>Identify key areas for process improvement</li><li>Train financial staff on new procedures</li><li>Spot check financial records after 30 days to ensure compliance</li><li>Retrain as necessary</li></ul>	You should know what to do here. Don't get wordy. Use bullets.

Proposal Section	Example Response	Rationale
Time per week	Four hours per week	We recommend half-day increments (e.g., 4, 8, 12, 16 hours). Any more than 16 hours per week will likely interfere with your job search and other activities – avoid higher-commitment engagements.
Term of engagement	Three months beginning Dec. 1	Typical engagements last between three and nine months. Anything longer than that, and they might need an employee, not a contractor. You can consider becoming an employee at that point...if you decide that's what you want.
Hourly rate	$150	This is an optional section! It's better to start at the monthly rate because...

Proposal Section	Example Response	Rationale
Monthly rate	$2,500	...the client can more easily compare this to hiring a full-time person. $2,500 per month equals $30,000 per year. Do you think they can hire a CFO-level person for that? No way. Make sure to mention that in your verbal (not written) conversation.
Total / Term	$7,500 for the full three months	This is another optional number (if they insist). Businesses typically think about consultants on a month-to-month basis. The big number can get scary.

Proposal Section	Example Response	Rationale
Billing terms	Net 30*, electronic transfer *Due 30 days after the invoice date. You can set any number you like. 30 days is pretty standard.	Make it clear how you expect to be paid. Most bank accounts allow for electronic transfer – set that up. Never wait for a check if you can avoid it!
Client authorization	Signature/Date	All of this should fit on one page. At the bottom, leave the signature block open. We'll talk about other paperwork you may want to consider in Chapter 9.

Bottom line: Do. Not. Make. This. Complicated.

Why you'll fit so well

Potential clients don't think about contractors the way they think about employees. For an employee, it's about "culture" and "fit" and "team dynamics." For a contractor, it's all about problem-solution fit. Let's have one last look at what makes Martha attractive as a consultant.

Rejection Points	Attraction Points
The client worries about full-time employee issues: fit with the team, fear of getting the hire wrong, growing healthcare costs, matching Martha's price to value over years.	The client doesn't have to worry about full-time dynamics. Martha brings solutions to the problem immediately, Martha costs less, and Martha isn't a long-term risk. That's attractive.

KEY TAKEAWAYS FROM CHAPTER 7

This one is easy. As a consultant you aren't selling your past or your personality. You are simply selling your ability to solve big problems the client can't solve themselves. Most people find this to be quite a relief. There's no bragging here. No ego. No uncomfortably long pitches. This is a get-down-to-business type of world. What about fit, culture, and personality? These come later...if at all.

Notes from the trail... Roger Lumpp

Understanding Your Client's Point of View

As demand for labor gradually outpaced the supply of labor over the past five years, hiring managers were forced to leverage alternative hiring methods to fill their positions. Gone were the days when a candidate had to check all the boxes to even be considered and the client held all the hiring power. As clients opened themselves to alternative hiring methods, the contract/consult-to-hire option gained acceptance opening a window for talent to take a try-before-you-buy strategy to their job search.

Contract consulting has a different cadence to it than full-time work. The pace of work is often more intense and demands a proven resource to get up the learning curve quickly. If you are a builder, fixer, and problem solver who is self-motivated you are going to enjoy contract consulting. On the flip side, if you are used to a more balanced cadence in your workday, contract consulting may not be the best path for you.

When clients come to the market for a consulting/project/interim/fractional resource it is for one of three reasons:

Deadline Driven: they have an urgent need for an audit, system go-live, compliance filing, trade show, etc.
Project Driven: they need a skill set they don't have in-house for a project but don't want/need to hire full time.
Business Stabilization: they had someone quit, take a leave of absence, and/or they are entering a period of extreme growth.

Historically, clients do their best to absorb this extra stress on their organization before resorting to the contract labor market. As a result, clients end up coming to market late in the game which contributes to the urgency of the hiring process and of the contract work itself.

If you are presented with a contract-to-hire opportunity, the interview process is going to feel different from a permanent hire scenario. The focus of a contract interview is on the present value of your skill set and how they map with the client's immediate need. The questions are going to be laser-focused on what needs to be accomplished in the next two to three months, which is very different from the behavioral questions in a permanent hire interview which are focused on fit over the next two to three years. To nail the "contract" part of the "contract-to-hire" scenario you need to stay focused on the short-term needs of the client, even if you are asked about your long-term career goals.

*Note: You may get a question about your long-term career goals and here is the ninja way of answering, "Ultimately I am looking for an organization where I can contribute on a full-time basis, but right now I want to help you and your team through this short-term challenge." You can't get the "to-hire" part of the journey without winning the "contract" part!

Most workers who are built for consulting prefer company environments where there are a lot of building, fixing, and optimizing opportunities. This could be a company in high-growth mode with an expanding org chart, a turnaround opportunity, or bringing two companies together through acquisition. If you are a consultant considering a conversion to a permanent position after a contract period, it is important to look at where the company is going over the next two to three years. If there is not enough interesting work ahead where you are going to be fully engaged and able to bring your whole self to work, you are going to get bored. Make sure you consciously evaluate the opportunity in front of you and make sure it's the right play for your career goals.

ROGER LUMPP
Professional Gig/Freelance Economy Expert
Creator & Host of "The Next Pro Gig" Podcast
773.909.8670
rogerlumpp3@yahoo.com

08

Easy sales techniques.

"Life is really simple, but we insist on making it complicated."
   - CONFUCIUS

The only thing worse than thinking about how to talk about ourselves...is actually talking about ourselves. Yuck.

It's hard enough to go through the job search process of resume writing and uploading, writing emails, and updating your LinkedIn profile. The thought of doing all of that and then having to sell yourself, face-to-face, as a consultant, amplifies that anxiety.

Part of that is our fault. By "our," I mean the coaching industry and its books. To make things seem more valuable, the job search industry loves to design complicated sales processes. We insist that you should become sales experts – have pipelines, processes, and psychological mastery. You have to know Google's search algorithms and be able to navigate ten different talent applicant tracking systems. Is it any wonder the job search is a leading cause of anxiety?

Keep it simple and you win.

Think about it for a second: How many consulting opportunities do you really need to get you through? Two? Three? You don't need to become an expert salesperson for this. You don't need to know code and algorithms. You don't need to become a LinkedIn superstar. To consult your way to a full-time job, you simply need to learn the right things about sales to get you through this phase and ignore the rest.

Put it another way: Do you need to be a mechanical engineer to drive a car? No. But is it useful to know how to pump gas or change a flat tire? Yes.

We're going to teach you the sales equivalent of pumping gas. You can handle it. We'll pause for a moment to remind you that the previous chapter taught you how to approach sales with a clear value of what you offer and an honest, humble, and giving way to approach it.

Here are the TOP FIVE quick sales techniques that we've found to deliver results in the minimum time.

Sales Technique	Why It Works
Call your current and past business colleagues and ask directly if they have consulting opportunities. Do they have a problem that needs solving?	People want to help. If they don't have an opportunity for you directly, ask them to make an introduction to someone else who might.

Sales Technique	Why It Works
Approach small and mid-size employers who are posting job opportunities. Contact the hiring manager and ask them to consider you as a short-term consultant to tackle the problem they are trying to solve faster.	Don't do this with large organizations – there are too many layers of bureaucracy to make it a "quick" technique (although it can work). Smaller organizations (a) often don't know what they need because they don't have the expertise to evaluate candidates, (b) will struggle to attract top talent at all, and (c) are more flexible to different ways to solve a problem.
Network with other existing, successful consultants outside of your skill set. They need to know you exist.	No, these are not competitors – even if they do what you do. Many opportunities come from partnering with another consultant who doesn't have the time to work on a project or doesn't have the specific expertise.
Connect with connectors. They know things you don't, and they want to know what you know.	There are people in your network who tend to be unusually "social" (see Chapter 6). Prioritize connecting with these people. They tend to know where opportunities are hidden because people like to talk to them.

Sales Technique	Why It Works
Personalize your pitches with video. People like to see faces and hear voices.	It's easy to add video to emails with today's technology, and plenty of services allow you to do it. It allows people to get to know you a little. Who people know, they tend to trust. (That's especially important when they don't know how to evaluate your skills!) Who they tend to trust, they tend to hire as consultants... and eventually, employees.

KEY TAKEAWAY FROM CHAPTER 8

Consulting your way to a full-time job is all about focus. Remove all the extra stuff you don't need. Focus on the techniques here that you do need. Do that, and you are well on your way to consulting your way to a full-time job.

You don't need a complex sales system to secure a few consulting gigs to bridge you to a new career. Simply focus on executing a few techniques well.

Notes from the trail... Lynn Hargreaves

"But I'm an introvert, not a salesperson!"

As an introvert, I used to believe that I couldn't succeed as a consultant because the idea of having to "become a salesperson" felt overwhelming.

Turns out, I didn't need to become anything other than myself in order to be successful. I just needed to reframe the conversation in my own head to be about listening and learning about what challenges the other person is facing. Now that I can do!

If you're anything like me, though, you may not be sure where to begin with leading that conversation. Don't worry; it's not rocket science. But sometimes having a framework makes it easier to get started. With that in mind, here are a series of questions that I've found work well to uncover the problem and determine the value the client places on fixing it:

- **"How's business?"** You'll learn: what's on their mind and why they're interested to talk with you.
- **"What challenges are getting in the way for you?"** You'll learn: specifics that will help determine if your skills are a fit to help them.
- **"How long has that been a problem?"** You'll learn: how entrenched the problem is and how strongly they feel about it.
- **"What's the impact of that on your business?"** You'll learn: what the problem is costing them (in money, time, quality, etc.) which translates into the value of fixing it.
- **"What have you tried to address this so far?"** You'll learn: how much effort they've already put into fixing it and what tactics they've tried.
- **"Why is now the right time to fix this?"** You'll learn: the level of urgency they have around taking action and their timeline to fix.
- **"What's your budget?"** You'll learn: what number they have in their head and whether it's in the ballpark of what you charge.

With these questions answered, you'll have a good sense for whether or not you can help them, how serious they are about paying for help, and whether they can afford your services. If it seems like a match, you can then follow up with your written proposal outlining the specifics of how you will help.

And just like that, fellow introvert, you're "doing" sales!

LYNN HARGREAVES (she/her)
Strategies that Get Done
Hargreaves Consulting, Inc.
www.hargreavesconsulting.com

09

Your business system.

"Your days are numbered. Use them to throw open the windows of your soul to the sun. If you do not, the sun will soon set, and you with it."
- MARCUS AURELIUS, *The Emperor's Handbook*

Up until this point, we haven't talked about the basic "business necessities" – how you set up your business with the state you live in, how you account for taxes, how you set up a new LinkedIn page, etc. There's a reason we ordered the chapters as they are, with basics only appearing now.

Most books and advice on this subject start with simple basic things in mind...and it's a mistake. A big one. Like any big idea, you need to start with the big stuff first – things like knowing the value you offer and being able to communicate it quickly, knowing who is likely to need you, and knowing your earning power. Imagine building your dream home starting with the second-floor bathroom sink soap holder. You would never do it that way. Start with the big stuff first.

We've seen too many people spend weeks on basic tasks while they should be looking for consulting clients first. You don't need to worry about handling the business issues until you have a client and you're getting paid. In other words, you don't have to do the basic tasks first. In fact, you shouldn't.

Still, the time comes when they do need to be done.

The trick is to keep it simple. Check off just the very basic basics and consulting your way to your next full-time job will be a far simpler journey.

Remember, the point of your "business" is to bridge you through to your next full-time job. That might be anywhere from three months to one year. You're not inventing the next Amazon or U.S. Steel. You are simply creating a reliable revenue stream in your interim job stage. We know even that sounds daunting. As always, we've made a nice little cheat sheet here you can use.

Basic tasks you need to complete to consult your way to your next full-time job*

Setup Task	Approach
Business setup with your state	Your state's secretary of state office will have plenty of assistance for you. Check with them as the rules will vary by state. Most of the time you simply need to register your business to get an Employer Identification Number (EIN) that separates your business from your personal Social Security Number (SSN). It's a necessary step that will take an hour or two at most. In my home state of Minnesota, the cost is just $135. Well worth it.
Taxes and Accounting	Find a CPA (Certified Public Accountant) and get professional tax advice based on your situation. Don't try to wing it if you haven't done this before.

Setup Task	Approach
Legal	Consider a subscription to a service like Legal Shield, where you can ask simple legal questions for cheap. A monthly fee runs around $39. Super affordable.
Health Insurance	If you don't have health insurance through a spouse or partner, we recommend (at least) purchasing a catastrophic policy. You can also purchase good insurance on the open market. Catch and other online resources cater to consultants for benefits.

Our own very affordable lawyers tell us this is the place to point out that we're not lawyers, we're not accountants, and we're not insurance providers. We don't know your specific situation, so we can only provide general guidance and encourage you to take it from there. Get qualified tax, legal, and health insurance advice. It's not as expensive as you may think.

KEY TAKEAWAYS FROM CHAPTER 9

The bottom line here is don't ignore the business basics, but don't focus on them too much either. Having a bona fide business will feel good, but it's only small progress toward your goal in the larger picture. It's just a ticket to the game.

1. Do the important stuff first. Figure out your value proposition, network, and approach potential clients.
2. Do the business setup stuff only when you have a client ready to go.
3. Don't fall into the basics trap. Basics are easy so they attract attention. But they don't pay the bills so tread lightly on them. Here's a rule of thumb: If everything on this list takes more than four hours, it's too long.

10

Managing your four-part schedule.

"Happiness can be found even in the darkest of times if one only remembers to turn on the light."
- ALBUS DUMBLEDORE

What?! A four-part schedule? I thought I was just looking for a job and doing some consulting work to bridge me to the next job? That's two parts! What's with the four parts?

Relax, it's okay. This will make sense. Besides, when in your career have you ever had less than four things on your plate? Exactly! Context is everything, isn't it? Here are your four parts.

JS = Job Search (your formal, full-time job search)
CO = Consulting Opportunities (searching for consulting work)
EM = Earning Money (doing the work for your consulting clients)
SS = Staying Sharp (keeping yourself mentally and physically fit)

We choose these four parts because we know that most people struggle to compartmentalize their time. Most people will recognize that searching for consulting work and doing consulting work are two different things and can put them in a box and check them off. But people often fail to recognize the value of #4 (physical and mental fitness) enough to build it in as equal priority to the other three.

Allow me to riff on #4 for a moment, because it really, really matters. It has to do with your mindset. Mindset is everything. #4 is your inoculation against the wrong mindset. You can follow all the specific advice in this book, but if you don't believe you can consult your way to a full-time job (because you're frustrated, depressed, or angry), or you physically can't do it (because you're physically ill or injured), you are not likely to succeed.

You must make time for all four aspects of your new, albeit temporary, professional life. And the best way to do that is to schedule that time!

The following is an example from Jamie. Jamie is on the hunt for a new Operations Management position. Here's how Jamie organizes his day:

Time	Activity	Code
Wake up (6:00 a.m.)	No sleeping in. Stay on schedule.	SS
6:30 a.m.	Healthy, consistent breakfast	SS
7:00 a.m.	Plan the specific activities and tasks for the day.	CO
7:30 a.m.	Take a 30-minute walk (outside or at the gym, weather dependent).	SS
8:30 a.m.	Scan job postings and target employers. Make notes for new applications and outreach.	JS
9:00 a.m.	Networking call (20 minutes) and thank you note (10 minutes)	CO
9:30 a.m.	New LinkedIn networking outreach for consulting opportunities	CO

Time	Activity	Code
10:30 a.m.	Meeting time with a consulting client on-site to address quality issue on the shop floor	EM
1:00 p.m.	Healthy lunch	SS
1:30 p.m.	Reading time (he enjoys science fiction)	SS
2:00 p.m.	Client project	EM
2:30 p.m.	Craft 1:1 strategies with 10 new job postings. Send customized video outreach.	JS
4:30 p.m.	Craft email proposal to new potential consulting client.	CO
5:00 p.m.	Close the laptop.	SS

KEY TAKEAWAYS FROM CHAPTER 10

You need to structure your day much more intentionally than you probably have done before. In fact, as you look back at previous jobs, you may notice that a lot of your day was structured for you, and not in ways you may have chosen.

Remember the four parts to your day:

JS= Job Search
CO=Consulting Opportunities
EM=Earning Money
SS=Staying Sharp

Be very careful about spending time outside of those four parts!

11

Now...begin!

"Get busy living, or get busy dying."
- ANDY DUFRESNE, *The Shawshank Redemption*

By reading this book to this point you now have everything you need to create a bridge for yourself to your next full-time position – a bridge that not only provides financial stability, but also professional dignity. With the skills you now possess, simply by reading this book and following our simple guidance, you are in a far better position than you'll ever be doing a traditional job search. Never again will you settle for the first job that comes along and accept whatever they're willing to pay. You know your worth now. You are aware of your options. You are patient, not panicked.

In this book, you've learned to dispel the most common mental roadblocks holding you back from the professional life you deserve. The lies you tell yourself in darker moments no longer hold you back.

The lie that you don't have the "right" skills.
You have all the skills you need and more – plus the wisdom to use them.

The lie that you don't know the "right" people.
You can easily build a robust network that will serve you.

The lie that you don't have the "right" frame of mind.
You now have the confidence to demand better for yourself.

In our second year of building Voyageur U, I wrote down five truths about consultants in my journal. They came from session after session of coaching as I tried so hard to help people understand that their worth is higher than ever. These five truths have been in every email I have sent out from that day forward:

1. Your value is in your wisdom.
2. Your value is in your objectivity.
3. Your value is in your scars.
4. Your value is in your viewpoint.
5. Your value is in your failures.

Now, all you need to do is...*begin.*

The Trailhead For Your Independent Career

Are you ready to make consulting your full-time career? Do you want to design a work life that fits in better with your "life" life? A Voyageur U membership might be right for you.

Voyageur U is for professionals who wants to chart their own career path. After all, the world of consulting and freelancing is the new normal. We provide a plan to get you started on your journey and a community to sustain you on your way. Membership includes enrollment in our 100+ lessons teaching you to continue to grow your business and improve your outlook on your career.

Everything is covered in our lessons. From how to pick a good accountant and lawyer, to setting up healthcare for yourself and loved ones. We also cover personal branding, client management, even sales tactics to land your first gigs.

Voyageur U can help you on your professional journey — whether you're new to independent work or looking to elevate your gig work to the next level. We believe that the business you want is achievable with the right education and the right community.

We support you all the way.

Get access to all training resources and our networking community for only $19/month.

Why go independent? You'll be joining the ranks of more than 33% of the American Workforce. One in three workers has realized that full-time jobs for seasoned professionals have a shelf life of under three years. That's not anyone's idea of job security. Operating independently diversifies your income streams and mitigates risk.

Join Us Today at www.VoyageurU.com

About the Author: John Arms

Like most people who will read this book, John Arms hacked his way through the job market jungle. In 2018, After a 25-year career as a business executive, CEO, and business owner, John chose to chuck corporate life to pursue an intense curiosity in the gig economy (aka fractional work, aka consulting, aka freelance, aka you get the picture).

As luck would have it, John found Jason Voiovich, a kindred spirit with the same curiosity in the gig economy. Together, they launched Voyageur U, a training ground for people coming out of corporate America seeking to become successful fractional executives and consultants. Little did they know that in the next two years the world would see a global pandemic, a great recession, offices closing their doors worldwide, a great resignation, and a complete reshuffling of the way we work – a reshuffling that, at printing time of this book, is still trying to form itself into something new.

In addition to his duties at Voyageur U, John is also a guest speaker, writer, podcaster, fractional CMO, and advocate for the independent professional workforce.

You can reach John on LinkedIn or via email at
John.Arms@VoyageurU.com

Made in the USA
Monee, IL
05 April 2023

31367992R10046